A fashionable HISTORY *of* MAKE-UP & BODY DECORATION

A FASHIONABLE HISTORY OF MAKE-UP &
BODY DECORATION
was produced by

David West 🧍🧍 **Children's Books**
7 Princeton Court
55 Felsham Road
London SW15 1AZ

Author: Helen Reynolds
Editor: Jackie Gaff
Picture Research: Carlotta Cooper
Designer: Julie Joubinaux

First published in Great Britain in 2003 by
Heinemann Library, Halley Court, Jordan Hill,
Oxford OX2 8EJ, a division of
Harcourt Education Ltd.

OXFORD MELBOURNE AUCKLAND
JOHANNESBURG BLANTYRE GABORONE
IBADAN PORTSMOUTH (NH) USA CHICAGO

Copyright © 2003 David West Children's Books

07 06 05 04 03
10 9 8 7 6 5 4 3 2 1

ISBN 0 431 18330 9 (HB)
ISBN 0 431 18338 4 (PB)

British Library Cataloguing in Publication Data

Reynolds, Helen
A fashionable history of make up and body
decoration
1. Cosmetics - History - Juvenile literature
2. Body marking - History - Juvenile literature
3. Fashion - History - Juvenile literature
I. Title II. Make up and body decoration
391.6'3'09

Printed and bound in China

PHOTO CREDITS :
Abbreviations: t-top, m-middle, b-bottom, r-right,
l-left, c-centre.

Front cover m & 10l, tl & 12bl, r & 18l and
pages 5tr, 6br, 10br, 11tr, 12tl & r, 16tr, 17tl &
tr, 20-21, 23l, 24tl, 25r & 26bl – Mary Evans
Picture Library.
Pages 3, 4br, 5br, 6-7t, 16bl, 19bl, 24tr & b, 25tl –
Dover Books. 4tr, 6tl & bl, 9tr, 22br, 26r, 28bl, 29r
& b – The Culture Archive. 5l, 7 all, 8ml, 9bl &
br, 11tl & br, 13tl & br, 14l & tr, 15tl & br, 17bl,
18tr, 19tr & br, 20tr, 21 & br, 22bl, 23br, 25bl,
27tr & br, 28-29 – Rex Features Ltd. 8tl – The
Kobal Collection/BFI/United Artists. 14-15 – The
Kobal Collection/ICON/Ladd Co./Paramount. 8bl –
Hulton Archive. 11b – Corbis Images. 13tr, 27l –
Digital Stock. 20tl – ISG113867 A Young Lady of
Fashion (oil on panel) by Paolo Uccello (1397-
1475), Isabella Stewart Gardner Museum, Boston,
Massachusetts, USA/Bridgeman Art Library. 22tr –
(LDBDA s236 – Elephant ivory dentures featuring
human, or 'Waterloo' teeth, and human teeth
strung together for sale, 1815-20) & m (LDBDA
s301 – "A French dentist shewing a specimen of his
artificial teeth and false palates", 1785, Thomas
Rowlandson caricaturing Nicholas Dubois de
Chémant) – British Dental Association Museum
Collection.

Every effort has been made to contact copyright
holders of any material reproduced in this book.
Any omissions will be rectified in subsequent
printings if notice is given to the publishers.

*An explanation of difficult words can be
found in the glossary on page 31.*

A *fashionable* HISTORY of MAKE-UP & BODY DECORATION

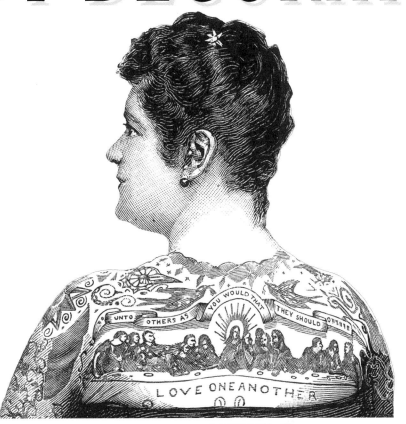

Heinemann
LIBRARY

Contents

5 From eye-paint to illustrated skin

6 The eyes have it

8 Lovely lips

10 The painted face

12 Finishing touches

14 Painted bodies

16 Body scarring & piercing

18 Tasty tattoos

20 The body beautiful

22 Tooth & nail

24 Hairy faces

26 Natural beauty

28 Mass markets

30 Timeline

31 Glossary

32 Index

ANCIENT ADORNMENT

Women and men were beautifying themselves with make-up back in ancient Egyptian times.

MAKING A LASTING IMPRESSION

Although the tattooist's art is at least 5,000 years old, its revived popularity in the West dates from the 1760s. Illustrated men and women with the kind of all-over tattoo shown below were popular exhibits at fairgrounds and circuses in the early 19th century.

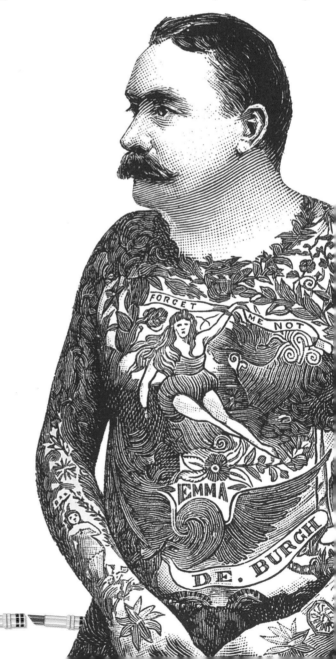

From eye-paint to illustrated skin

A STROLL DOWN A BUSY STREET in any of the world's major cities will today reveal countless variations in face and body decoration. Most people now take experimenting with their appearance for granted. The presence or absence of make-up is widely accepted, as are tattoos and body piercing. Body decoration is not a modern phenomenon, however, and it has meant different things in different cultures throughout history. Among other things, make-up has been employed as a badge of social status and to proclaim membership of a group. Above all, though, it has been used to enhance beauty, with every era setting its own standard of fashionable perfection.

Make-up for the masses

In the 1920s, mass production made cosmetics more widely available.

Cutting a fine figure

Fashions in facial hair have fluctuated over the years. In the early 1900s, the stylish Edwardian swell sported a big, bushy moustache.

Home-cooked beauty aids

Caring for the skin has always been as important as covering it up with make-up. Recipes that use kitchen-cupboard ingredients to whip up face packs and skin ointments have been around since ancient times.

The eyes have it

EYE-PAINTS DATE BACK TO ANTIQUITY *and originally may have been used as a form of magical eye protection. By ancient Egyptian times, however, vanity had taken over and eye-paints were used by both men and women as beauty aids.*

Mice in the make-up box

Ideas about eye beauty changed over the centuries, with some bizarre practices coming and going. In the 18th century, for instance, fashionable women shaved off their eyebrows and applied artificial ones made from mouseskin!

EGYPTIAN BEAUTY SECRETS

Egyptian eye-paints were made from minerals ground into powder. Eyes were either outlined in kohl made from black galena (a lead ore) or with green malachite (a copper ore).

ELIZABETHAN EYESORE

Queen Elizabeth 1 (1533–1603) used drops of the poisonous deadly nightshade plant (below) to make her pupils larger and her eyes appear more brilliant. Fashionable women continued this practice for centuries afterwards.

NEW TAKE ON AN OLD LOOK

This American magazine feature illustrated the 1960s fashion for Egyptian-style eye make-up in heavy kohl pencil.

By the 19th century, the obvious use of make-up was frowned upon and it was only worn by the kind of women considered disreputable, such as actresses and prostitutes. The early 20th century saw huge changes in women's lives, however, and an accompanying shake-up in acceptable behaviour.

The short hair and cloche hats of the 1920s flapper girl drew attention to the face. Eyes were highlighted with an eyebrow pencil and coloured eyeshadow, as well as lashings of dark mascara.

In the following decades the emphasis was more on the lips, but as skirts shrank in the 1960s, eyes became big again – literally. Mini-skirted chicks accentuated their eyes with opalescent eye shadow, false eyelashes and thick, black eyeliner.

CLOSE EYE CONTACT

Coloured and patterned contact lenses (above) were a late 20th-century introduction – another way of emphasizing the eyes.

MODEL MAKE-UP

With her dark, heavily made-up eyes, pale lips and short, geometric haircut, the fashion model Twiggy (Leslie Hornby b.1949) was the epitome of 1960s glamour.

LUSCIOUS LASHES

Although at their most popular in the 1960s and 1970s, false eyelashes have been around since the early 1900s.

Painted Men

In the 18th century, upper-class men and women wore elaborate make-up, including lip-paints made from ground-up plaster of Paris with added colourings.

Pretty Boys

The 1980s saw a general trend towards glitz and glamour. In subcultures such as the New Romantics, men and women wore lashings of bold make-up, including dramatic lipstick.

Rebel, Rebel

Although during much of the 19th century make-up was frowned upon, from the 1890s onwards, suffragettes campaigning for votes for women sometimes adopted red lip-paint. It was a symbol of their defiance of traditional ideas about acceptable female behaviour.

Lovely lips

LIP-PAINT IS ANOTHER BEAUTY AID that dates back to ancient times. Neatly packaged lipsticks weren't available in those days, of course, and cosmetics were made by the wearer or a servant. The ancient Egyptians ground up an earth called red ochre, while the Greeks mashed up seaweed and mulberries.

Nature & artifice

Bold use of lip-paint went in and out of vogue over the years. Roman women loved bright lips, for example, while in the Middle Ages a more natural look was preferred.

In 17th- and 18th-century Europe, lip-paints were used by the nobility of both sexes, as a mark of their social rank. After the French Revolution of 1789–99, however, Europe was swept by a new passion for simplicity in clothing and general appearance. Men stopped wearing lip-paint, and there was a sharp decline in its use by women which continued throughout much of the Victorian era.

Lip stuff

The twist-up lipstick in a metal tube was a 20th-century introduction. Before then, lip-paint mainly came in pots and was applied with the finger or a brush.

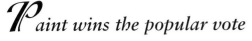

Paint wins the popular vote

By the early 20th century, discreet lip-paint was again being used by society ladies. Lip-crayons had been around since the 16th century, but most lip-paints came in pots, were greasy and needed a deft hand to apply them. In 1915 the first lipstick in a sliding metal tube was patented. This easy-to-apply product was an immediate success and was soon being manufactured in a range of red tints. By the 1920s the wearing of lipstick was commonplace among stylish women, and has remained so until the present day.

Red for victory

New clothes were in short supply during World War II (1939–45), so women used make-up to boost morale and add glamour to their lives.

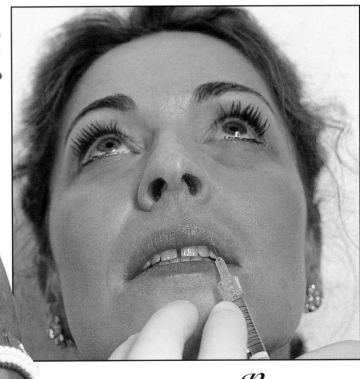

Big is beautiful

Lip-paint isn't the only way of drawing attention to the lips. In some cultures (left), huge plugs are used to stretch them. In others (above), people have their lips injected with a substance called collagen.

The painted face

IN THE WESTERN WORLD *up until the early 20th century, pale skin was a sign of wealth and status. Suntans were abhorred, as they were associated with outdoor work and the labouring classes. Anyone who was anyone painted and powdered their face the palest shade of white.*

Dicing with death

Smallpox scars were commonplace until a vaccine for the disease was perfected in the late 1790s, and face make-up was also used to cover spots and scars.

Recipes for whitening the skin and hiding blemishes were around in Roman times. Although some ingredients were harmless, others such as powdered white lead were definitely dangerous. The effects of lead poisoning began with headaches, nausea and stomach cramps. The worst cases could end in paralysis or death.

East meets West

At times, white face-paint has also been worn by non-White cultures. It is still a part of the traditional make-up of the Japanese geisha.

Elizabethan elegance

Like other noblewomen of her day, Elizabeth 1 whitened her face with a thick layer of toxic, lead-based paint.

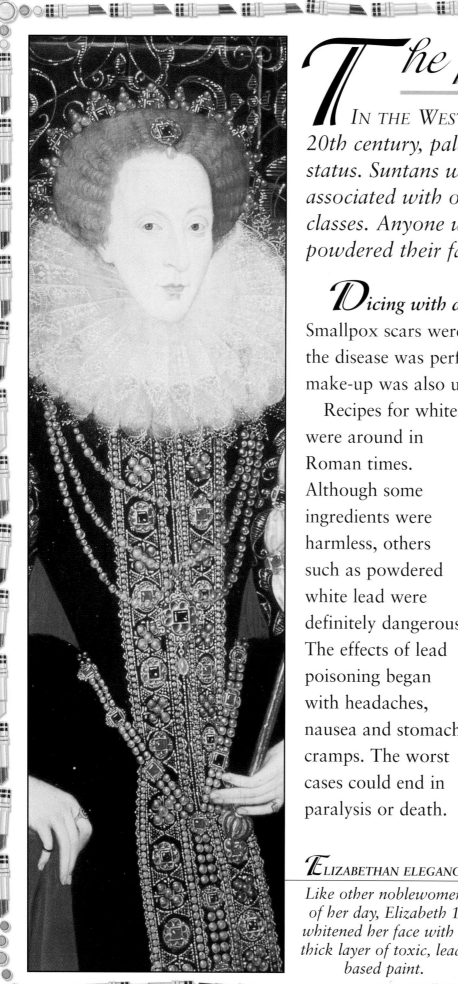

Masked beauty

Early 20th-century cosmetics such as Max Factor's Pan-Cake brand coated the skin and created a rather mask-like effect. The skin tones were naturalistic, but the look was almost as artificial as the white face-paint of earlier eras.

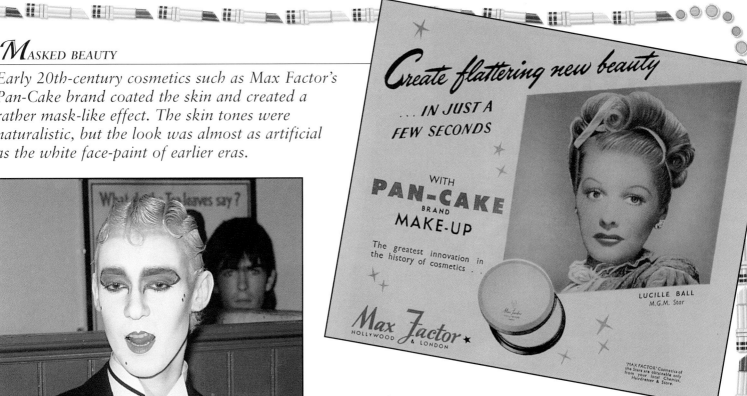

Create flattering new beauty ... IN JUST A FEW SECONDS WITH PAN-CAKE BRAND MAKE-UP

The greatest innovation in the history of cosmetics ...

LUCILLE BALL
M.G.M. Star

Max Factor
HOLLYWOOD & LONDON

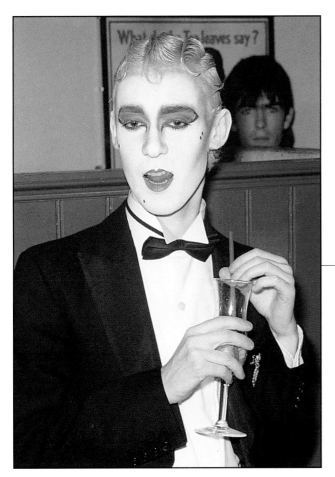

Ghostly white

Although flesh-coloured make-up has dominated fashion since the early 20th century, the white-faced look has sometimes resurfaced, such as in the look of the New Romantics of the 1980s.

Ending the cover-up

It wasn't until make-up fell from favour in the 19th century that the use of harmful products such as white lead declined. When make-up came back in vogue in the early 20th century, a more natural look became stylish and women began wearing flesh-coloured cosmetics. Early foundations and powders still tended to cover up the skin, creating a heavy, matt surface. It wasn't until the 1980s that sheerer, more light-reflective products became available.

Painted warriors

Face-paints have long been used in war – either as a very visible message of defiance (above) or to camouflage soldiers (left) and help them blend into the background.

Finishing touches

NOWADAYS WE USE BLUSHER to give cheeks a rosy glow. In the 17th and 18th century, noblemen and women smeared on a red paste called rouge, to create a look that to modern eyes appears more feverish than healthy.

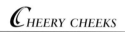

Cheery cheeks

No 18th-century lady's make-up was complete without a liberal application of rouge.

Patching over the cracks

Smallpox scars and other blemishes were hidden beneath black patches designed to look like natural beauty spots. In 18th-century Britain, patches were also used by the nobility to indicate which political party they supported. Tories wore patches on their left cheek, while their opponents, the Whigs, wore them on the right.

Desperate measures

To achieve a fashionable pallor, some Victorian ladies resorted to having themselves injected with dangerous substances peddled by quack chemists.

A passion for patches

Originally used to cover blemishes, beauty patches became more elaborate in the 18th century and were cut into stars, hearts and other shapes.

HOLY MARKER

In countries such as India it is traditional for Hindus to make a coloured mark on the forehead as a sign of piety. In the past, married women often wore red marks, while unmarried ones had black marks. Today, the marks often match the colour of the woman's sari.

PUNK PATTERNING

In the 1970s, punks took the art of face decoration to new extremes, using everything from paints to piercing.

NATURAL BEAUTY

In the 1950s, women used eyebrow pencils to copy the natural beauty spots of film stars Marilyn Monroe (1926– 62) left, and Elizabeth Taylor (b.1932).

From pallor to perfection

By the 1790s the passion for patches was fading, while only older women and actresses continued to apply rouge. For much of the 19th century it was fashionable for ladies to look 'pale and interesting', with only a slight pink tinge in the cheeks – a state that was induced by avoiding fresh air and dubious practices such as drinking vinegar.

The revived popularity of make-up in the early 20th century was accompanied by a renewed interest in rouge, which was now considerably lighter in both colour and consistency and often came in powdered form.

Painted bodies

BODY PAINTING WAS PROBABLY THE EARLIEST FORM of *human artistic expression, along with cave art. It was practised by a diverse range of cultures and on most continents, from the Americas to Australia. We cannot be certain why prehistoric people developed this art, but one reason may have been to mark momentous occasions in life.*

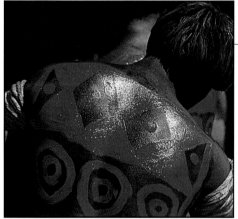

ALL DRESSED UP

In some cultures body paint is seen as a form of clothing – people would feel naked without it.

TIMELESS TRADITION

Body art has deep spiritual significance for the Aboriginal peoples of Australia, and many communities have their own unique patterns.

Rites of passage

Body art may have been used to mark a person's death and departure to the afterlife, for example, or to give symbolic protection when undertaking a difficult hunt or journey. Traditionally, the paints were made out of berries, bark, leaves and earths such as red and yellow ochre, which were ground and then mixed with vegetable oils or animal fat.

Art & society

In some cultures, body art was seen as a way of distinguishing humans from animals. It was also used as a sign of social rank, and to separate one tribe from another.

Other cultures have practised body art for different reasons. Face-painting has long been an essential part of the circus clown's art, for instance, while performance artists have been using their own bodies as a canvas since the late 1960s. For children, having their face painted like an animal or a pirate is just part of the fun of dressing up, and face-painting stalls are now a frequent sight at fêtes and shopping centres.

Hippie protest

In the 1960s, some hippies adopted body paint in order to differentiate themselves from mainstream Western society.

Blue funk

The Celtic peoples of ancient Britain made a blue body paint from the leaves of the woad plant. They used it to make themselves look even more terrifying in battle, as seen on Mel Gibson in Braveheart (1995).

Brown study

In India (right) and North Africa, the plant dye henna has been used for centuries to create highly elaborate body art for weddings and other ceremonies. Henna is now often used for temporary tattoos.

Body scarring & piercing

MORE PERMANENT THAN BODY PAINTING, scarring and piercing have also been practised for centuries. The reasons for these body arts varied between cultures, and included marking social rank or the passage into adulthood.

Making a lasting impression

Scarring techniques differed, but they often involved scratching patterns into the skin with a sharp object such as a stone or a shell. An irritant such as wood ash was then rubbed into the cuts so that raised bumps and ridges were left after the skin healed.

MARKED MAN
Although rarely done today, body scarring was traditional among Australian Aboriginals.

Taking a piercing interest

Body piercing was far more widespread than scarring, and it was carried out on virtually every part of the body. The ornaments that were inserted were made from metal, bone, shell, ivory or glass. In ancient Egypt, even cats wore earrings. Lip-plugs were worn by the Mayans of ancient Mexico and the Inuit of Alaska. Nose-rings have long been traditional in India, Pakistan and many other countries.

NOSING AROUND
Piercing the septum, or centre of the nose, was most common among warrior cultures. Nose-plugs could be as thick as 2.5 centimetres.

BATTLE SCARS

Until the beginning of the 20th century, German university students settled quarrels by fighting sword duels. Duelling scars were a sign of manhood and were worn with pride.

SOCIAL STIGMA

In Europe, branding scars were used to set criminals apart from the rest of society from ancient times to the early 19th century.

Ringing the changes

In mainstream fashion, over the past few hundred years, earrings were the most common reason for body piercing. It was no surprise, then, that people reacted with shocked horror in the 1970s, when punks began piercing other body parts with safety-pins. The shock didn't last long, however, and nose, eyebrow, lip, tongue and navel piercing is now widely accepted – and widely practised by young people the world over.

TAKING A TIP FROM ANCIENT HISTORY

When punks took up multiple ear-piercing, they revived a practice that archaeological evidence shows was around 4,000 years ago.

Tasty tattoos

TATTOOING IS ANOTHER PERMANENT FORM OF BODY ART, *a cross between painting and scarring. Patterns are made by pricking tiny holes, through which coloured pigments seep into the skin. In the past, tattoos were done by hand, using a sharp stick, bone or needle. In the early 1890s, the practice was revolutionized by the invention of the electric tattoo machine.*

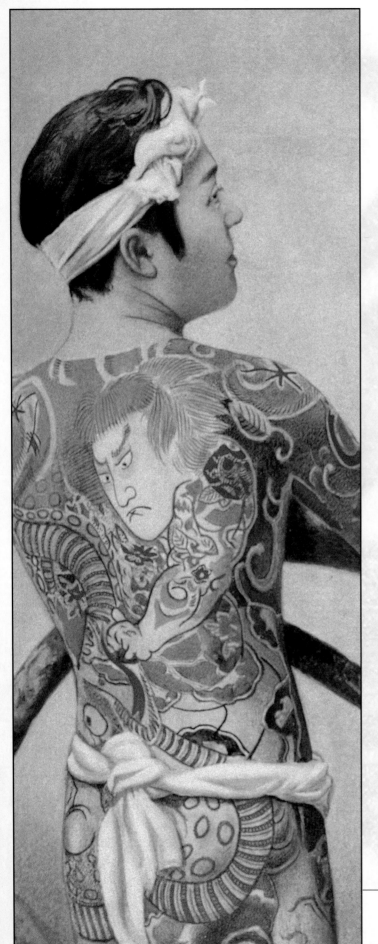

Nifty needles

Modern tattoo machines can make as many as 3,000 tiny holes per minute.

Icemen & mummies

Like other forms of body art, tattoos have meant different things to different cultures, from the purely decorative to signpointing high or low social status. One of the oldest-known examples of tattooed skin was found on the body of Utzi the Iceman, who died more than 5,200 years ago in the Alps mountains between Italy and Austria. Tattoos have also been discovered on 4,000-year-old Egyptian mummies.

The art of the Japanese tattooist

In Japan, tattooing began to flourish as an art form in the 18th century. Inspiration for the elaborate images came from woodcuts and watercolours.

Temporary tattoos

Henna is not the only form of temporary tattoo, stick-on tattoos are also available. They usually last for one to two weeks.

Sailors & pop stars

In the West, interest in tattoos was revived by the voyages of Captain James Cook (1728–79) into the Pacific during the 1760s and 1770s. Fascinated by Pacific customs, some of Cook's crew were themselves tattooed and began a trend among sailors. Tattooing is now seen as a skilled art form, particularly as practised in Japan and by the Maoris of New Zealand – and is enjoying a revival, especially among young people.

Maori messages

Called Ta Moko, the traditional Maori tattoo records a man or woman's family history as well as their tribal status.

Roll up, roll up

Although common among Western sailors by the early 19th century, tattoos were seen as highly exotic by most landlubbers. Tattooed women and men were a popular exhibit at fairgrounds and circuses, and people paid good money to gasp and stare.

Preparation makes perfect

Modern tattooists usually work out complex designs like this on paper. A stencil is used to transfer the design and act as a guide when tattooing.

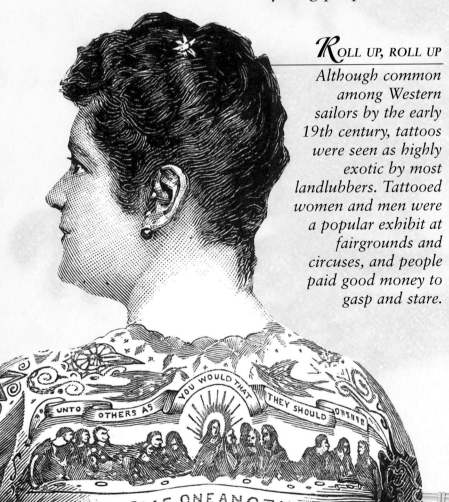

UNTO OTHERS AS YOU WOULD THAT THEY SHOULD

LOVE ONEANOTHER

During the 15th century, European noblewomen shaved their hair and sometimes their eyebrows to achieve a fashionably high forehead.

The body beautiful

IN EACH CULTURE AND ERA, *people have had different ideas about beauty. In the West in the late 19th century, for instance, women used corsets and bottom-enlarging bustles to create voluptuous S-shaped curves. In the 1920s and 1960s, the stylish women's figure was boyishly flat-chested.*

Bound head & foot

In some cultures, the pursuit of the perfect body shape led to more permanent changes. In China, until the custom was banned in 1911, young girls' feet were bound to restrict their growth to as little as 8 centimetres. In some African and North American communities, the practice of head-shaping dates back hundreds of years.

HEAD START

In the past, the Chinook people of northwestern North America practised head-shaped by strapping their childrens' heads between wooden planks.

NECK BANDS

Among the Padaung tribe of Burma, an elongated neck was considered beautiful for women. Gold or copper neck-rings were added over a period of time to stretch the neck.

*B*IG IS
BEAUTIFUL

*While some
people spend
their lives dieting
to reduce their
body size, others
spend most of
their time
exercising to
increase it.
Body builders
treat their bodies
rather like a
living sculpture,
building up
muscle strength
and size through
weight-training
and exercise.*

*C*utting & tucking

Today, the craft of the plastic surgeon has
put ancient body-shaping techniques in the
shade. It is now possible for people to have
virtually every part of their body altered.
Excess fat is removed through a technique
called liposuction, breasts are enlarged,
entire faces are reshaped and wrinkles are
treated with Botox injections. By far the
most widespread surgical enhancement,
however, is the facelift. In an era in which
youth is seen as all-important, an increasing
number of women and men are regularly
submitting their faces to the scalpel.

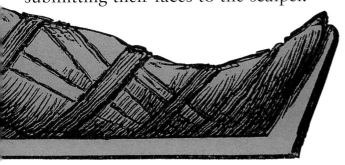

*P*LASTIC FANTASTIC

*Like many stars, the American singer
and actress Cher (b.1946) has undergone plastic
surgery, having her nose reshaped and her face lifted.*

Tooth & nail

MANY A BEAUTY'S SMILE WAS MARRED by rotten or missing teeth before the 19th century, when modern dental science began to develop and people began to understand the causes of tooth decay. In the past, the cheapest solution was to have rotten teeth extracted – an excruciatingly painful business before anaesthetics were invented in the 1840s.

Teething problems

The first-known sets of false teeth were made in Italy around 2,700 years ago, by the Etruscans. The use of dentures had died out by the Middle Ages, however, and when they were reintroduced in the 17th century, only the wealthy could afford them. More ornamental than practical, early dentures often fell out and had to be removed when eating.

What a mouthful

Early false teeth were carved from animal bone, ivory or mother-of-pearl, or cast in silver or gold. Human teeth were also used – pulled from the dead or sold by poor people from their own mouths.

Cultural differences

Not everyone thinks that even, glistening white teeth are beautiful. In parts of Africa and Southeast Asia, teeth are filed into sharp points or dyed different colours.

Mouth jewellery

Decorating teeth with precious jewels is not a new custom. Hundreds of years ago, the Mayan people of South America inlaid their teeth with turquoise and jade.

Hands-on experience

Throughout history, clean hands and buffed, filed fingernails were considered a sign of the leisured upper classes. At times it was also fashionable for the aristocracy to show that they didn't dirty their hands with work by growing extremely long nails.

Nail varnish didn't come on to the market until the mid-1920s, when it was sold alongside the new, mass-produced make-up. Open-toed sandals became fashionable at this time, and women started to paint their toenails. In the 1930s, it became stylish to co-ordinate nail varnish and lipstick colours.

The 1980s was the age of power dressing, and no well-groomed career women looked complete without immaculate nails. Once a service offered only by hair salons, manicure parlours sprouted in high streets and shopping malls, offering everything from a lunchtime retouch to a full set of false nails.

FAKING FINE FINGERNAILS

Although artificial nails didn't become a fashion accessory until the 1970s, they were marketed to nail-biters as early as the 1930s. These days they're available in a range of colours and decorations.

Hairy faces

MEN'S MOUSTACHES AND BEARDS have come and gone over the centuries. Ancient Egyptian men were usually clean-shaven, for example, although beards were fashionable from time to time.

Splitting hairs

In ancient Greece, in contrast, beards were usual until the 5th century BCE, after which they were mainly worn only by old men and philosophers as a sign of their freedom from worldly concerns. The Romans were obsessed with a clean shave, and no man's day was complete without a morning visit to the barber. Viking men, on the other hand, wouldn't have been seen dead with a beard.

When beards and moustaches were in, men often rang the changes by altering their shape. For the noblemen of medieval Europe, for instance, a neatly trimmed and waxed forked beard was stylish for many decades.

FACIAL FALSIE

Like other ancient Egyptians, pharaohs were usually clean shaven. However, part of their royal regalia was a false beard tied around the chin with a strap.

MAKING A POINT

Upturned moustache tips and a goatee beard were all the rage in the first half of the 17th century.

VICTORIAN VALUES

As the 19th century progressed, luxuriant facial hair came to symbolize the Victorian ideals of seriousness and sobriety. The second man from the left's sideburns were a new fashion.

Holy hair

Full facial hair has long been a sign of piety in many religions, from Judaism to Sikhism.

A close shave

In the periods when beards were out, men suffered for the sake of a smooth chin. For centuries, the only practical razor was the cut-throat (a long blade with a handle), and shaving accidents were a daily hazard. The breakthrough in shaving technology came in 1901, when American King C. Gillette (1855–1932) patented the first safety razor with a disposable blade. The final step towards facial freedom came in the 1920s, with the invention of the electric razor.

Designer stubble

In the 1980s, film and pop icons such as singer George Michael (b.1963) set a trend for designer stubble.

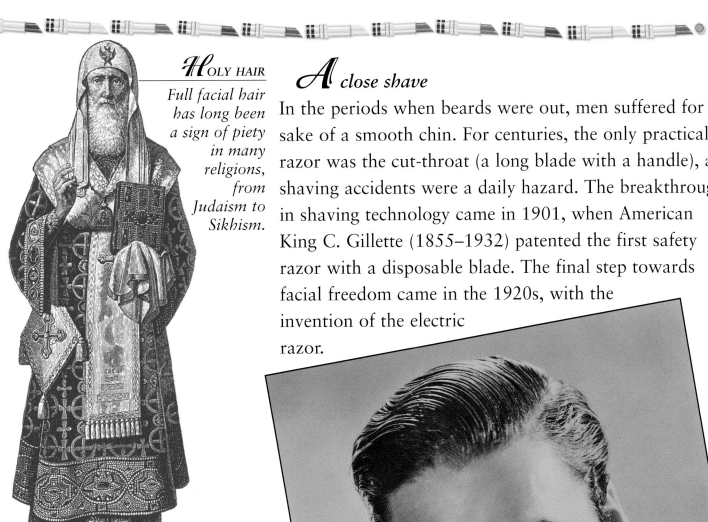

Lip style

A pencil-thin moustache became a must for men in the 1930s, after the style was sported by movie stars such as the swashbuckling Errol Flynn (right, 1909–59) and the suave Clark Gable (1901–60).

Natural beauty

IN THE 1920S, AFTER CENTURIES OF PALLOR, *the suntan became fashionable in Western society. The style guru Coco Chanel (1883–1971) is said to have inspired the change, when she accidentally became tanned after falling asleep in the sun.*

Soaking up the sunshine

The dangers of the sun's ultraviolet rays and the risks of skin cancer weren't widely understood in those days, and for decades sunbathers focussed on acquiring a tan as quickly as possible, not on protecting their skin. For those who couldn't afford holidays in hot countries, fake tans and sunlamps were soon being offered as alternatives.

Sunny side up

Early sun care was designed to increase the chance of a tan or to soothe burned skin, not to protect it from the sun's ultraviolet rays.

Full coverage

Even at the seaside, it was usual for the Victorian woman to cover every inch of her body with clothes and to carry a parasol to protect her fashionably pale complexion from the sun.

Staying in the shade

Effective sunscreen lotions became available in the late 1970s. By the 1990s, health agencies were warning people to protect themselves from the risk of skin cancer by covering up, using sunscreens and avoiding sunbathing. Fake tans have become increasingly sophisticated, as people continue to pursue the feeling of health and well-being today associated with a tan.

Fitness fanatics

The 20th century also saw a growing obsession with exercise. One of the earliest promoters was Irishwoman Molly Stack (1883–1935), who in 1930 founded the Women's League of Health and Beauty with the aim of improving the health of the ordinary woman. Aerobics took off in the 1970s and the fitness industry is now big business, with centres offering everything from t'ai chi to step classes.

NATURAL LEADER

In the 1970s Anita Roddick (b.1942) pioneered, with great success, cosmetics made from natural, environmentally-friendly ingredients.

THE NATURAL LOOK

Once the icon of grunge, supermodel Kate Moss (b.1974) has been famous for her natural-looking make-up since the mid-1990s.

LET IT BURN

Millions of women and men are today members of gyms or health and fitness clubs. Hours are devoted to gruelling exercise routines in order to shape and tone the body beautiful.

Mass markets

WHEN THE FIRST MODERN BEAUTY PARLOURS opened in the 19th and early 20th centuries, the focus was on skin care not on make-up, which was only just becoming respectable. Two famous pioneers were Helena Rubenstein (1870–1965), who opened a salon in London in 1902, and Elizabeth Arden (1884–1966), who opened her first New York salon in 1909.

Home brews

From ancient Egyptian times (right) until the 19th century, beauty tools and cosmetics were made by hand, often in people's homes.

Maxfactorize your own beauty

FOR THAT STAR-LIKE LOOK OF LOVELINESS

★ Share this glamour secret of Hollywood's most alluring screen stars, and *maxfactorize* your own beauty with famous *Max Factor Hollywood* Make-up in the correct shades which are individually prescribed to enliven, enhance, and harmonize perfectly with the natural colourings of your hair, eyes, and complexion. Try it . . . for a thrilling adventure in new beauty.

BETTY HUTTON
STAR OF PARAMOUNT'S "DREAM GIRL"

COLOUR HARMONY MAKE-UP

MAX FACTOR Cosmetics of the Stars are obtainable from your local Chemist, Hairdresser & Store

created by

Max Factor
HOLLYWOOD

From movies to mass production

Mass-produced make-up was a spin-off from the newly born film industry, and its founding father was Max Factor (1877–1938). Working in Hollywood in the 1910s, Factor started by concocting make-up that looked natural under the harsh lights of the movie camera. The success of these products led to his famous Pan-Cake make-up, which went on sale to the general public in the 1920s. Rubenstein and Arden followed rapidly with their own ranges.

Stars in their eyes

Max Factor became famous as make-up artist to the stars, and one of his most successful advertising ploys was to use photos of well-known movie actresses to endorse his products.

Growth of an industry

Unlike the dangerous, lead-based cosmetics of earlier centuries, modernday beauty products are devised by chemists and subjected to rigorous safety tests before they are released on to the market. Hundreds of ingredients are now available, including a cocktail of chemicals, as well as natural dyes and oils, beeswax, petroleum and talcum. Today, make-up is on sale virtually everywhere, from the local corner shop to the supermarket. Make-up artists undergo professional training, and the cosmetics industry is a multi-billion pound business.

MOVIE MAGIC

Make-up artists devised special masks to help transform actor John Hurt (b.1940) for the 1980 film The Elephant Man. *The quality of their work led to the establishment of a Best Make-up category in the 1981 Academy Awards, when it was won by* An American Werewolf in London.

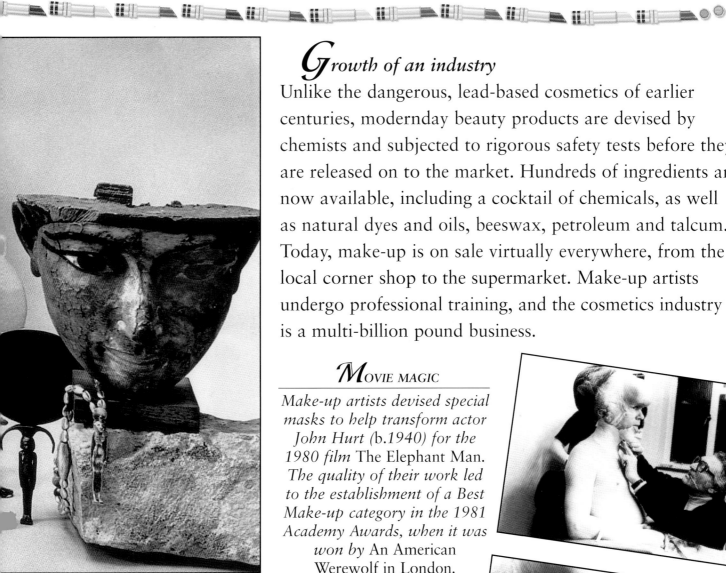

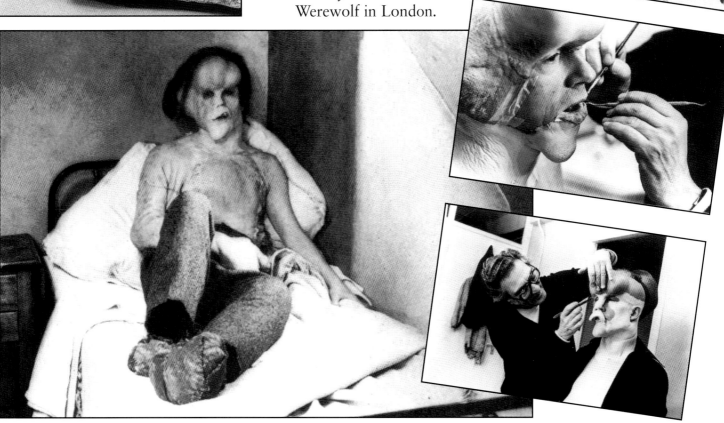

Timeline

Prehistory

Paintings on cave walls reveal that people were adorning their bodies with coloured paints many thousands of years ago. Tattooing, scarring, piercing and other permanent forms of body art developed from body painting. Various forms of body art were practised by different cultures worldwide. The earliest physical evidence of tattooing has been found on the 5,000-year-old body of Utzi the Iceman.

The ancient world

In the ancient civilizations that developed around the Mediterranean, the hot climate demanded relatively simple clothing which was compensated for by elaborate make-up. In Egypt, noblemen and women used a range of home-made skin and hair care preparations, as well as tinted face, eye and lip make-up. Greek and Roman women also used make-up, which included a face-paint made from poisonous white lead. The earliest-known sets of false teeth were made in Italy about 700 BCE by Etruscan dentists.

The Middle Ages

The Christian church preached against make-up, calling it devilry. The boldest women of nobility continued to use lip-paint and rouge discreetly. In France, women used wheat powder to whiten their faces. In South America, Mayan nobles inlaid their teeth with precious stones.

16th century

The Renaissance period saw a flowering of new ideas in art, architecture and literature, and the beginnings of modern science. In the European royal courts, clothing and make-up became more intricate and sumptuous. Noblewomen made up their faces heavily, colouring their eyes, lips, cheeks and even, sometimes, their teeth. White lead was employed once again as a face-paint, and drops of deadly nightshade were used to make eyes sparkle.

17th century

Noblewomen carried on applying their make-up liberally. Pale skin continued to set the nobility apart from the working classes, and to symbolize aristocratic wealth and leisure. While the poor had rotten teeth extracted, the rich had theirs repaired with gold or lead fillings or replaced by false ones made of bone, ivory or metal.

18th century

Heavy face make-up was worn by upperclass men as well as women, and white lead still formed the usual basis of face cosmetics. Tiny black patches were used to cover up blemishes such as smallpox scars. Eyebrows were sometimes shaved off and replaced with false ones made of mouseskin. Captain James Cook's voyages introduced his sailors to Pacific tattooing practices, sparking a revival of interest in tattoos in the West.

19th century

A passion for simplicity swept Europe in the aftermath of the French Revolution (1789–99), causing extravagant make-up to give way to a more natural look. By the 1850s, obvious make-up was associated with actresses and prostitutes. Chalk and talcum had by now replaced white lead in cosmetic preparations.

20th century & beyond

As women began to gain new freedoms such as the right to vote, attitudes towards make-up became more liberal. Commercial ranges of cosmetics began to be widely available in the 1920s, and suntans became fashionable. Red lips were the focus of the face for several decades. In the 1960s cosmetics companies targeted a younger market, and heavily made-up eyes and pale lips became stylish. Make-up became sheerer and more light-reflective in consistency. In the last 25 years, there has been a renewed interest in body painting, tattooing and piercing.

Glossary

Body piercing

Making holes in the body in order to insert ornaments such as ear- and nose-rings.

Botox

A brand name for the chemical botulinum toxin, which is injected as a cosmetic treatment for wrinkles and other lines.

Branding

Making an identifying mark, usually by burning it into the skin with a scalding hot iron tool. Cattle and criminals have been branded since ancient times.

Collagen

The substance collagen occurs naturally in the skin and other tissues, where it helps maintain strength and elasticity. Cosmetic injections of collagen are used to make lips fuller, and to treat facial lines.

Cosmetics

Beauty products such as face make-up, which are designed to enhance appearance or provide skin care.

Foundation

A cream or lotion smoothed into the skin as a base for face powder.

Goatee

A pointed beard, allowed to grow on the front of the chin only, and named because it looks like a goat's beard.

Henna

A reddish-orange dye obtained from the leaves of a shrub. In North Africa and Southeast Asia, henna has been used for centuries to colour women's hair, hands, nails and feet, as well as to dye mens' beards and horses' hooves and manes.

Ochre

A red or yellow kind of earth, which has been ground up and used as a pigment since prehistoric times.

Plastic surgery

A branch of medicine concerned with the surgical repair or reshaping of the body. Plastic surgery is not only used to enhance beauty, but to treat injuries such as burns.

Sideburn

A line of hair allowed to grow down below the ears. Sideburns were named after the American General Ambrose E. Burnside (1824–81), who popularized the style.

Tattoo

A coloured design or picture created by making thousands of tiny needle-pricks into the skin and allowing permanent dyes to seep into the holes.

Index

Aboriginals 14, 16
Arden, Elizabeth 28

beard 24–25
beauty patch 12–13, 30
    salon 28
    spot 13
body art 14–21, 30
    building 21
    painting 14–15, 30
    piercing 5, 16–17, 31
Botox 21, 31
branding 17, 31

Celts 15
Chanel, Coco 26
Chinook 20
collagen 9, 31
contact lenses 7
cosmetics 5, 6–13, 23, 26,
    28–29, 30–31

Egyptians 4, 6, 8, 16, 18,
    24, 28, 30
Etruscans 22, 30
eye make-up 6–7, 30

facelift 21
face make-up 10–13, 30
Factor, Max 11, 28

false beard 24
    eyelashes 7
    nails 23
    teeth 22, 30
film industry 28–29
fitness 26–27
Flynn, Errol 25
foot-binding 20
foundation 11, 31

geisha 10
Gillette, King C. 25
goatee 24, 31
Greeks 8, 24, 30

head-shaping 20
henna 15, 31

Japan 10, 18–19
jewellery 16–17

kohl 6

lead, white 10–11, 30
liposuction 21
lipstick 8–9, 23, 30

make-up artist 29
Maoris 19
mass production 28–29
materials 6, 8, 10, 14, 22, 29
Mayans 16, 22, 30
Michael, George 25
Monroe, Marilyn 13

Moss, Kate 27
moustache 5, 24–25

nails 23
nightshade, deadly 6, 30

ochre 8, 14, 31

plastic surgery 21, 31

razor 25
religion 13, 25, 30
Roddick, Anita 27
Romans 8, 10, 24, 30
rouge 12–13, 30
Rubenstein, Helena 28

scars 16–17, 30
sideburns 24, 30–31
smallpox 10, 12, 30
special effects 29
Stack, Molly 27
suffragette 8
suntan 10, 26–27, 30

tattoo 4–5, 18–19, 30–31
teeth 22, 30
Twiggy 7

Victorians 7, 8, 12, 24, 26
Vikings 24

warpaint 11
woad 15